A WORSHIP HANDBOOK

MUSICIANS
IN THE ASSEMBLY

Robert Buckley Farlee

AUGSBURG FORTRESS / MINNEAPOLIS

Book design: Richard Krogstad
Cover art: Jane Pitz
Editors: Dennis Bushkofsky, Rebecca Lowe

Manufactured in the U.S.A.   ISBN 0-8066-4279-3
08 07 06 05 04 03 02 01   1 2 3 4 5 6 7 8 9 10

CONTENTS

Musicians in the Assembly

This booklet is intended for all who serve as leaders of church music in congregations. The title "musicians in the assembly" covers quite a bit of territory—from those who work with multiple choirs, large instrumental programs, and a large salaried staff, to those who are fortunate to have half a dozen singers on a Sunday and be accompanied by an old piano, and for all who are in between. Across that whole spectrum, though, church musicians have some things in common:

- They rejoice when the song of God's people is raised up, in whatever form it takes.
- They covet more of those rare moments of self-forgetful praise or unhindered musical meditation.
- They see themselves not as stars of the show, but as servants of the body of Christ.
- They realize that there is always more to be learned about leading God's people in song.

This booklet will try to address some basic issues of the why and how of serving as a musician in a congregation. This resource is by no means an exhaustive treatment of the subject, but rather a primer, touching on some of the essentials. The concluding bibliography will point you toward more detailed resources.

What is laid out here is not intended to be the only right way to approach church music. But if you are looking for a way to faithfully address the bullet points above, this is a starting place.

Above all, thank you. Yours is a challenging task, one that is often under-appreciated and occasionally fraught with conflict. Yet it is a profoundly vital task, for what would the church be without song?

Lutherans and Church Music

The Lutheran church has always placed music on a high plane. It has held the nickname "the singing church" because of its rich heritage of chorales and hymns. This high regard for the people's song originated with Martin Luther himself. In one preface to a collection of motets, Luther wrote:

> I would certainly like to praise music with all my heart as the excellent gift of God which it is and to commend it to everyone. But I am so overwhelmed by the diversity and magnitude of its virtue and benefits that I can find neither beginning nor end or method for my discourse. . . . Looking at music itself, you will find that from the beginning of the world it has been instilled and implanted in all creatures, individually and collectively. For nothing is without sound or harmony. . . . And yet, compared to the human voice, all this hardly deserves the name of music. . . . Next to the Word of God, music deserves the highest praise.
>
> *"Preface to Georg Rhau's* Symphoniae Iucundae" *(Luther's Works 53:321-323)*

If Luther was impressed with the diversity of church music in the sixteenth century, what might he think today? Recently the Lutheran church has tried to reach out to many traditions and cultures, incorporating a variety of musical contributions. By opening up to a wider range of musical styles and traditions, the Lutheran church has tried to become less parochial and more accepting of the catholicity of the whole church.

Being open to new musical styles, however, does not mean that the Lutheran church no longer has anything particular to say about church music. Lutheran theology is firmly grounded in God's word—especially in the good news of God's work through Jesus Christ. The Lutheran understanding of church music is no exception. From the time of Luther to the present day, Lutherans have held music to be so important that its place in the church is clearly defined—not so that people will not try new things—but so that music will be focused on serving God.

The Evangelical Lutheran Church in America has adopted a statement called *The Use of the Means of Grace* that includes a section articulating the approach to church music. Under the heading "The Arts Serve the Word," the following principle is set forth:

Music, the visual arts, and the environment of our worship spaces embody the proclamation of the Word in Lutheran churches

(*The Use of the Means of Grace,* Principle 11).

An application to this principle states:

Music is a servant of the Gospel and a principal means of worshiping God in Lutheran churches. Congregational song gathers the whole people to proclaim God's mercy, to worship God, and to pray, in response to the readings of the day and in preparation for the Lord's Supper.

(*The Use of the Means of Grace,* Application 11A).

There is much to consider in what that statement includes and what it omits. For instance, the statement does not define a type of music suitable for the church (such as classical music, contemporary song, or country western). While people all have preferences, it is important that music of whatever style be "a servant of the Gospel." Church music is not an end unto itself. Rather, it is a means to proclaim the gospel of Jesus Christ.

Music, whether vocal or instrumental, is a bearer of God's word to those in need. Just as God's word often speaks against our common assumptions, so does the music that serves God's word. Pleasing the greatest number of people should not be of primary consideration when evaluating music. Instead, church musicians should be concerned about what music can best serve God at that particular moment.

Notice the words "congregational song" in application 11A from *The Use of the Means of Grace.* The congregation is the center of all church music. Yes, worship services may include an organ toccata, a guitar riff, or a choral motet, but the central goal of musical efforts in the church is to enable the song of God's people. All else is secondary in the application of the church musician's efforts.

The verbs in application 11A give church musicians plenty to work with in planning music that will serve the people: gather, proclaim, worship, pray, respond, and prepare. These are all worthy roles for music to play. Every piece of music will not meet all of them, but within an entire worship service the music can serve each of those functions.

Each church musician takes his or her place in a line that stretches far back in time. For Lutherans, that line can be traced back through people such as J.S. Bach, Martin Luther, Gregory the Great, Ambrose of Milan, and the Biblical figures Mary, David, and Miriam. From that line the Lutheran musical heritage can be expanded outward to include countless people of nearly every heritage. Now, as Lutheran church musicians stand to lead God's people in song, some of the challenges are new, while many more challenges are old. Nevertheless, the goal remains the same: to give voice to praise of the one who alone is worthy of being praised.

Putting It into Practice

Lutheran worship and church music have a liturgical heritage, as compared to denominations that use freer worship forms. Liturgical, however, does not mean stodgy. Lutheran worship at its best includes music as an integral part of the worship. Certain parts of the liturgy are normally reserved for the song of the people. These moments of song are not breaks in the liturgy, but important pieces of the whole. At other points a choir, cantor, or other musicians may speak on behalf of the people. It is important to remember that no one is ever merely a spectator at worship. In an entertainment-oriented society, leaders of church music are given the responsibility to help all people get involved in the church's song.

Though Lutheran music has its roots in northern Europe, it is not limited to music from European-American cultures, such as Gregorian chant or Scandinavian choral music. Lutheran worship services may employ songs from many other cultures as well, such as the African call-and-response hymn or the Hispanic balada, as well as Western songs in more contemporary idioms. While some sounds may be new to worshiper's ears at first, after a period of committed use many people will become committed to a rich mixture of song.

If the goal is to help create vibrant worship, the watchword needs to be inclusive. This watchword should not mean promoting blandness. Instead, it should mean including as many people as possible both as participants and as leaders of music. Ask the following questions as you plan worship music: How can seniors be more involved? How about children and youth? Are gifts of both men and women well represented? The greater variety of voices heard, the better.

Nuts and Bolts

Each church music program enjoys different amounts of resources. Some music leaders can only hire an orchestra a couple of times a year, while many choir directors wish for just one good, consistent tenor in the choir. While many are stirred when large forces combine in God's praise, two people lifting up their voices is just as pleasing to God. With the appropriate planning, much can be done to provide worship music, regardless of the size of your budget.

CHORAL SONG

Vocal leadership is the heart of church music. This statement is not meant to minimize the ministry of instrumentalists, but rather to recognize that more people have voices than play instruments, and that words and music can only be combined vocally. So then, what sort of vocal leadership is appropriate? A key recommendation is to try for a choir, if at all possible. Do this not simply for the sake of the literature you can do—although that is certainly rewarding—but remember that the point of music in worship is to lead the congregation in song. A choir serves well as a sub-group and model within the congregation.

If your choir is small, it can actually motivate you to rethink the role of the choir. A choir performing Handel's *Messiah* is not the norm for church music, but rather the exception. Having the ability to sing a work of this magnitude is wonderful, but that is not what congregational music is all about. Instead, the primary duty of the congregational choir is to support the people's song. Assist the congregation in learning hymns and liturgical music. Alternate with the congregation in singing hymn stanzas or psalm verses. Support the congregation so all will have the courage to raise their own voices in song.

The choir's secondary role is to take primary leadership of certain parts of the liturgy. In a communion service, the congregation does not always have to sing the same alleluia verse before the gospel. Each Sunday and festival has an appointed acclamation for that day that the choir may sing. Several settings of alleluia verses are available for cantors and choirs, typically also with congregational refrains. The same is true for the offertory. Such verses and offertories are available in musical settings from a variety of publishers. See planning resources such as *Sundays and Seasons* (Augsburg Fortress, annual) to discover the breadth of possibilities.

While it is most appropriate for the congregation to sing the psalm, the choir may assist by alternating verses with the congregation, or by singing an appointed refrain or antiphon. Other parts of the liturgy, such as the hymn of praise or the "Lamb of God," should almost always be sung by the congregation rather than the choir. On special occasions, however, the choir might perform a more elaborate setting of one of those parts of the liturgy.

Singing an anthem on its own is secondary to the choir's leadership roles described above. Help the choir to understand its ministry (see "The Ministry of the Choir" on page 23, which may be reproduced and given to choir members), and try to focus on the liturgy in a creative and fresh way. When the choir does sing anthems, sing those that contribute to the service that day. Make sure that the music selected comments on themes in the scripture readings and helps the congregation enter into the spirit of the season.

SOLO VOICE

While a choir may be the best way to model song for the assembly, solo voices also have significant roles. Presiding and assisting ministers have vocal parts assigned to them in the liturgy, and musical leaders in a congregation may be called upon to assist them with these responsibilities. Assure presiding and assisting ministers that operatic-quality voices are neither necessary nor particularly desirable for that leadership. A simple, unforced voice will serve the purpose quite nicely. The recording *Singing the Liturgy* (Evangelical Lutheran Church in America, 1996) offers an excellent model.

Some parishes are blessed with vocalists who are willing, maybe even eager, to share their gifts with the congregation. The principles laid out for the ministry of the choir apply here as well. The main goal for a vocalist is to aid the congregation's song. Use the same list of priorities as presented for the choir, making adaptations where necessary. While a soloist may not be capable of assisting in the people's song to the extent that a choir can, it is important that the solo vocalist not be understood as putting on a performance for the congregation, but instead joining his or her voice to those of all who are gathered to praise God.

The role of cantor or song leader is more integrally related to the liturgy, designed to lead the people's song rather than present independent musical selections. If the cantor sings with humility (not necessarily softly), she or he may better be able to encourage the response of the congregation than if the cantor intimidates them with full-voiced sound intended to impress.

The cantor or song leader's ministry is often done in full view of the people. With simple gestures the cantor can indicate when it is time for the people to enter the song. Because the model of entertainer is so prevalent in our culture, the church song leader must take extra care to disassociate from it. Whether working alone or as part of an ensemble, the song leader is a servant, not a star.

In some cases, it will be necessary for the song leader to use a microphone. A cantor should not use a microphone as an entertainer by waving it around and drawing attention to it and its user. Similarly, if the amplification level is too high, it will bombard the congregation into silence; and the congregation will take on the role of an audience rather than a worshiping assembly. Set the sound level so that the singer can be heard clearly, but no higher.

INSTRUMENTALISTS

During certain eras in church history, sung scripture was thought to be the only music worthy for worship services. Now churches are much more open, recognizing music in general as a gift of God. Many forms of instrumental music are welcome in worship.

Typical opportunities for instrumental music are prelude, postlude, during the offering, and during distribution of communion. Instrumental music is not the only option for these moments, though. A choral piece can help prepare us for worship, as can silence. On some occasions, instruments may be used in place of voices. Try alternating stanzas of a hymn between different groups such as men, trebles, different sides of the nave, and so on. Another option is to let instruments play one stanza while no one sings, but everyone meditates on the text.

Organ

The organ may be the instrument most associated with the church. Organs work well to provide a sustained sound loud enough to be heard in the midst of a singing congregation. In addition, organs are capable of a wide variety of sounds, from the nasal, cutting reeds to the soft flutes and strings. The organ's various lengths of pipes (16', 8', and 4' stops) allows listeners to hear pitches at octaves above and below the actual keys that are played. The lower pitch provides a foundation for the congregation's singing, and the higher pitch helps the musical line to be heard above the singing. Organists need to be aware of how they might use this versatile instrument in imaginative ways. Many helps are available to the organist, from organ method books to resources such as *Leading the Church's Song* (Augsburg Fortress, 1999).

Because of the breadth and variety of musical literature available to organists, the temptation is always present to spend all the practice time polishing up yet another dazzling prelude or postlude, while leaving scant time for hymn and liturgy preparation. The song of the people, however, is the primary responsibility of the church musician. Hymns and liturgical music call for careful, creative preparation. Let them be the center of the practice, as they are of the worship.

Piano

While the piano and its electronic counterparts (keyboards and synthesizers) may not have an immediate identification with church music as the organ does, they work well for leading worship. Because these musical instruments may not be primarily associated with worship, it is important to consider how worshipers will perceive their use. Try to offer new music and new instruments in a way that is not distracting to worshipers.

In order to be heard above congregational singing, it can be helpful for the pianist to play the bass line in octaves or to play the right hand up an octave. This technique can be tiring to the ear if used all the time, but it can help reinforce singing at certain moments.

Instrumental Ensembles

The instrumental ensemble has a long and honored history in worship, dating at least as far back as the psalms in the Hebrew Bible. It is altogether fitting that instrumental ensembles be included in worship. An advantage with instrumental ensembles is that, like vocal choirs, they model the corporate nature of the church. Ensembles are people joining together to craft their praise. Instrumental ensembles should take care to support the assembly's liturgy without overpowering it, or acting as performers instead of musical leaders.

Contemporary music includes a vast array of styles and genres. Taizé-style song, jazz ensembles, and bands with guitars and a drum kit, while all contemporary, are different forms of musical expression. No matter which style of music or instrumental make-up of an ensemble, it is important that its music meet the goals set out near the beginning of this booklet, promoting "congregational song [that] gathers the whole people to proclaim God's mercy, to worship God, and to pray, in response to the readings of the day and in preparation for the Lord's Supper."

Music and Liturgy

No matter what style of music it is, by definition church music serves the church. It is music integrated into the liturgy. Even though many musicians are not experts in liturgical studies, it is important to put music and liturgy together in a way that forms them into a unified, naturally flowing worship service.

A good place to begin thinking about church music is to look at what is basic to worship. Within the Lutheran tradition, the eucharist or holy communion is the primary form of worship. Though in practice it doesn't always happen, Lutheran churches are encouraged to celebrate communion weekly (*The Use of the Means of Grace,* principle 35). Within that primary liturgy, we can see four large sections (A fifth section, when appropriate, is bath—that is, holy baptism). They are, in order:

GATHERING. This may include, after any pre-service music and order of confession, an entrance hymn or song(s), the greeting by the pastor, the Kyrie, a hymn of praise, and the prayer of the day.

WORD. The basic outline of this section is: first reading, psalm, second reading, gospel acclamation, gospel reading, sermon, hymn of the day, creed, and the prayers.

MEAL. This section begins with the greeting of peace, then proceeds through the offering of gifts (offertory), great thanksgiving (prayers and sung acclamations at the table), the Lord's Prayer, distribution of communion, a post-communion canticle, and a prayer.

SENDING. This is generally a short section, with blessing, perhaps a sending hymn, and a dismissal.

Church musicians and worship planners should keep in mind is that the above is an outline. Though some items are essential (the reading of the gospel and distribution of communion, for example), others may be expanded or eliminated. Within this overall outline, there is flexibility, with enough structure so the service can be generally familiar from week to week and congregation to congregation. While a service of word and sacrament may be a congregation's primary pattern of weekly worship, there are other forms of worship that may also be used, such as services of daily prayer.

How can churches put this shape of the liturgy to work? Instead of taking just any piece of music and placing it into some empty slot in the service, let the liturgy itself drive musical choices for the worship service. In the gathering rite, for instance, ask: Is this a festive day in the church year? If so, instead of a simple straight-forward entrance hymn, try a more festive setting of a hymn, or several praise songs, perhaps with a procession led by a dancer or two. After the greeting from the presiding minister on a festival day, try both a Kyrie (in one of many settings and styles available) and a hymn of praise ("Glory to God" or "This is the feast"). Or if it is a more penitential day (during Lent, for example), some quieter and more reflective music as the congregation gathers would be most suitable. In general, the gathering rite is a time for music of invitation and praise, but attuned to the rhythms of the liturgical year.

The liturgy of the word lends itself nicely to pieces that are based on scripture or that comment upon it. The psalm is normally part of the congregation's song, but a hymn paraphrase of a psalm can occasionally be substituted for the actual psalm. A choir anthem based on the psalm might also be sung. Additionally, a motet based on one of the readings can serve as a musical commentary. On special occasions, for example, one of Bach's cantatas or an equivalent work by another composer could expand on the psalm. The hymn of the day is the chief hymn of the service, and is a natural place to concentrate musical efforts. A more elaborate introduction might be employed for this hymn, while stanzas might be sung by different elements of the congregation in alternation.

Though baptism is not a weekly part of the liturgy, it is a fundamentally important event for the life of each individual and for the entire congregation. Inclusion of congregational or choral song at a baptism can help emphasize that this sacrament is centered on the church—of which we are all baptized members—and not on the individual being baptized. In congregations where baptisms ordinarily occur at baptismal festivals (the Easter Vigil, Pentecost, All Saints Day, and the Baptism of Our Lord), music related to baptism can be planned for these occasions.

Within the meal portion of the liturgy, the primary opportunities for music are around the offering and during the distribution of communion. Many parishes routinely schedule choir anthems during the offering. The offering may be an opportunity to try out other musical expressions, though. Perhaps an instrumental ensemble could offer musical gifts here. On certain occasions, particularly on Ash Wednesday or during Holy Week, silence may be best during the offering.

Music during the distribution of communion will be tailored to your own parish's needs and customs. Congregational song, particularly of a meditative nature, is common and appropriate. Hymns that use repeated, easily memorized refrains may be especially appropriate as people are moving about. The distribution is also a good time for a choral or instrumental piece. Do not be afraid of silence here either— many worshipers will appreciate it.

The word dismissal is related to mission. The sending rite does not require music, although often a postlude provides vigorous accompaniment as the assembly goes its way. The sending is when the worship service is ended, and it is the time for worshipers to go and serve the Lord in the world. Any music that is included during this rite could be related to the theme of mission and service.

Learning a New Congregational Song

Responding to the psalms, the church has always been singing new songs to the Lord. The current times have been as rich in new musical creations as any era. But it is still a challenge to find good new songs and to teach new songs to the assembly. The church musician should try to obtain access to several good hymnals.

Almost every Christian denomination has published major hymnals or supplements within the past couple of decades. In addition, independent publishers have issued collections in genres ranging from traditional hymnody to contemporary song. There is no need to restrict your explorations to a single denomination, although neither should you overlook the hymnal(s) regularly used in your congregation, since there may be unused gems just waiting to be discovered. In reviewing music that is available for a given day or season, you may come across hymns you would like to use at other times—make a note of these for future use. Pay attention to your criteria for choosing a new song. The text should be based on sound theology (ask your pastor to help you), while the music should be singable by a congregation, and an appropriate vehicle for the words themselves.

Once you have chosen a new song, you cannot add it to the repertoire of a congregation or a choir until you have obtained copyright permission (unless you have purchased copies of piece or a collection for everyone who will be using it). Unless the piece is old enough (both text and tune) to be in the public domain, you will need to obtain permission in order to reprint it on your own. Note that this needs to be done well in advance, because the publisher may require a written request and payment several weeks in advance. In rare cases you may be refused permission. Usually information about the copyright holder of a given text or tune will be printed underneath a hymn, or sometimes in the back of a volume in an acknowledgments section.

If further clarification about the holder of a copyright is necessary, you may often be able to contact the publisher of the hymnal or songbook. If your congregation holds one or more copyright licenses you may already have permission to reproduce a variety of songs, but be aware that no single licensing program covers all publishers. Also keep in mind that a copyright license offered by a publisher will generally apply only to material that it owns or administers, not to everything that it publishes (there is a difference). Make sure that you have the proper permission—it's the ethical thing to do!

When you are teaching a new song to the congregation, two things can be invaluable helps: the choir and repetition. Teach the hymn to the choir first and make sure they know it well. Let them sing it for the congregation for a week or two, then let the congregation sing it with the choir's help for a few weeks. When you decide to let a new piece rest, do not let it rest too long before you repeat it. Once a new hymn has been repeated regularly enough, it will become a natural part of the congregation's vocabulary.

Conclusion

We hope this brief overview of the church musician's ministry has provided encouragement and helpful information. No single book can hope to give you everything you need, though. On the following pages are additional resources that you may find useful, as well. They, in turn, can point you to additional helps. May God bless your important ministry of music!

PREPARING MUSIC

Cherwien, David M. *Let the People Sing!* Concordia Publishing House, 1997. A Keyboardist's Creative and Practical Guide to Engaging God's People in Meaningful Song.

Leading the Church's Song. Augsburg Fortress, 1998. A wide-ranging look at most genres of church music, with practical helps.

Parker, Alice. *Melodious Accord: Good Singing in Church.* Liturgy Training Publications, 1991.

Proulx, Richard. *Tintinnabulum: The Liturgical Use of Handbells* (rev. ed.). GIA Publications, 1997.

Singing the Liturgy: Building Confidence for Worship Leaders. Chicago: Evangelical Lutheran Church in America, 1996. A demonstration recording of the chants assigned to leaders in *LBW* and *WOV*.

Use of the Means of Grace: A Statement on the Practice of Word and Sacrament, The. Chicago: Evangelical Lutheran Church in America, 1997. Also available in Spanish and Mandarin versions.

Westermeyer, Paul. *The Church Musician* (rev.ed.). Augsburg Fortress, 1997.

———. *Te Deum: The Church and Music.* Fortress Press, 1998.

PLANNING TOOLS

Choosing Contemporary Music: Seasonal, Topical, Lectionary Indexes. Minneapolis: Augsburg Fortress, 2000. *Indexes for Worship Planning: Revised Common Lectionary, Lutheran Book of Worship, With One Voice.* Minneapolis: Augsburg Fortress, 1996. *Choosing Contemporary Music* provides references to multiple collections of contemporary praise and liturgical songs; *Indexes for Worship Planning* indexes the hymns and songs in *Lutheran Book of Worship* and *With One Voice.* Both include extensive scripture and topic indexes.

Sundays and Seasons. Augsburg Fortress. An annual guide to the church year containing an invaluable set of suggestions for church musicians, worship planners, and pastors.

Worship Books

Libro de Liturgia y Cántico. Minneapolis: Augsburg Fortress, 1998. A complete Spanish-language worship resource including liturgies and hymns, some with English translations.

Lutheran Book of Worship. Minneapolis: Augsburg Publishing House; Philadelphia: Board of Publication, Lutheran Church in America, 1978.

Lutheran Book of Worship, Ministers Edition. Minneapolis: Augsburg Publishing House; Philadelphia: Board of Publication, Lutheran Church in America, 1978.

This Far by Faith: An African American Resource for Worship. Minneapolis: Augsburg Fortress, 1999. A supplement of worship orders, psalms, service music, and hymns representing African American traditions and developed by African American Lutherans.

With One Voice: A Lutheran Resource for Worship. Minneapolis: Augsburg Fortress, 1995. Pew, leader, and accompaniment editions; instrumental parts, organ accompaniment for the liturgy, cassette.

Hymn and Song Collections

As Sunshine to a Garden: Hymns and Songs. Rusty Edwards. Minneapolis: Augsburg Fortress, 1999. Forty-six collected hymns with tunes by a variety of composers.

Bread of Life: Mass and Songs for the Assembly. Minneapolis: Augsburg Fortress, 2000. Jeremy Young's complete eucharistic music based on *With One Voice* setting five and twelve of his worship songs.

Dancing at the Harvest: Songs by Ray Makeever. Minneapolis: Augsburg Fortress, 1997. Over one hundred songs and service music items.

Global Songs 2: Bread for the Journey. Augsburg Fortress, 1997.

O Blessed Spring: Hymns of Susan Palo Cherwien. Minneapolis: Augsburg Fortress, 1997. New hymn texts set to both new and familiar hymn tunes.

Worship & Praise. Minneapolis: Augsburg Fortress, 1999. A collection of songs in various contemporary and popular styles, with helps for using them in Lutheran worship.

Other Hymnals and Hymnal Supplements

Borning Cry: Worship for a New Generation. Compiled by John Ylvisaker. Waverly, Iowa: New Generation Publishers, 1992.

Gather Comprehensive. GIA Publications, 1994.

Hymnal Supplement 1998. Concordia Publishing House, 1998.

Maranatha! Music Praise; Hymns and Choruses. Maranatha! Music, 1998.

The New Century Hymnal. The Pilgrim Press, 1995.

Praise and Worship Songbooks. Hosanna/Integrity Music, continuing series.

The Presbyterian Hymnal. Westminster/John Knox Press, 1990.

Psalter Hymnal. CRC Publications, 1987.

Taizé: Songs for Prayer. GIA Publications, 1999.

The United Methodist Hymnal. The United Methodist Publishing House, 1991.

Wonder, Love and Praise. A Supplement to the Hymnal 1982. Church Publishing, Inc. 1997.

THE MINISTRY OF THE CHOIR

You probably joined the choir because you love to sing. And you love to join your own voice with others to make music as you cannot do alone. Martin Luther described music as "an excellent gift of God." And we have been blessed who are able to share it with others. The purpose of music in the church is not to please ourselves, but it is to be in service to God and our neighbor. That said, the ministry of music will certainly be rewarding to those who perform it, as well.

How does music serve others? It may serve others when it helps them to contemplate God's grace and mercy shown through Jesus Christ. Music can serve other people when they hear a choir singing on their behalf, preparing and presenting music in a well-crafted manner. This presentation is certainly a worthy task for a choir to undertake. When we help members of a congregation to raise their own voices in song, however, we are performing our truest responsibility as a church choir. Worship is not a spectator activity. The psalms often speak about the work of the whole assembly: "In the midst of the congregation I will praise you" (Ps. 22:22). Similarly, the New Testament calls upon us "with one voice [to] glorify the God and Father of our Lord Jesus Christ" (Rom. 15:6). The point of assembling for worship is to engage all peoples' voices together in praise of God.

We have not reached our full potential as choir members until we have explored all of the ways we can help the congregation find its corporate and collective voice. Do we know the liturgy and hymns so we can support the worship of the entire assembly with rich, confident sound, giving all worshipers the courage to use their own voices? Where sung parts for the congregation are unfamiliar, can we model the singing for the entire assembly? Can we take appropriate portions of the liturgy (an alleluia verse, or parts of a psalm or hymn), so that our practiced choral tone is heard not as a musical performance, but integrated into elements of a whole liturgy?

To view the choir in such a servant role gives it a more significant place in the worship life of a congregation. The vision that we hold before us is not that of a small band of musicians gathered around the organ or piano, but something much more grand. As our communion is "a foretaste of the feast to come," so our song points to the whole company of heaven joining voices around God's throne. Let us as a choir support and enable all voices of the congregation so that no one may be left out of that great chorus!